J. RICHARD GENTRY

Step-by-Step Assessment Guide to Code Breaking

Pinpoint Young Students' Reading Development and Provide Just-Right Instruction

NEW YORK • TORONTO • LONDON • AUCKLAND • SYDNEY
MEXICO CITY • NEW DELHI • HONG KONG • BUENOS AIRES

The author and publisher wish to thank those who have generously given permission to reprint material:

Figures 10 & 22 from *Kindergarten Literacy* by Anne McGill-Franzen. Copyright © 2006 by Anne McGill-Franzen. Reprinted by permission of Scholastic Inc.

Figures 11, 19, & 20 from *Breakthrough in Beginning Reading and Writing* by J. Richard Gentry. Copyright © 2007 by J. Richard Gentry. Reprinted by permission of Scholastic Inc.

Figure 21 from *Nurturing Knowledge* by Susan Neuman and Kathleen Roskos. Copyright © 2007 Susan B. Neuman and Kathleen Roskos. Reprinted by permission of Scholastic Inc.

Figure 25 from Universal Publishing, *Nursery Rhyme Time: Reading and Learning Sounds, Letters, and Words* by J. Richard Gentry and Richard Craddock (2005 p. 4)

Figure 26 from Barbara Peterson. *Characteristics of Texts That Support Beginning Readers.* The Ohio State University. 1988.

::

Editor: Lois Bridges
Production editor: Amy Rowe
Video production: Jane Buchbinder
Video editing and DVD design: Maria Lilja
Cover designer: Maria Lilja
Interior designer: Sarah Morrow
Copy editor: Chris Borris

ISBN-13: 978-0-545-03602-3
ISBN-10: 0-545-03602-X

Table of Contents

::

Table of Contents for the DVD companion to
Step-by-Step Assessment Guide to Code Breaking by J. Richard Gentry

Introduction for Teachers

- An overview of phase and literacy development
- The five phases, at a glance

Richard Gentry's Assessment Interviews With Students

- Albert's reading and writing assessment (Phase 1)
- Kevin's reading and writing assessment (Phase 3)

Q & A With Richard Gentry

1. What do you consider to be the major breakthroughs in teaching beginning reading and writing?
2. What do you mean by phases, and how can I recognize a particular phase of development?
3. How does phase observation differ from other research-based stances in beginning literacy?
4. How does phase observation change our view of early intervention?

Downloadable Forms (reproducible assessment sheets)

Phase 0, Phase 1, Phase 2, Phase 3, Phase 4, Letters in Writing, Print Concepts, Prompts

Introduction

Have you ever considered the power of assessing children as you observe their responses to your instruction? The DVD that accompanies this guide shows me working with 4-year-old Albert and 5-year-old Kevin with a set of meaningful literacy activities, or "systems." I engage the boys with browsing boxes, story planning, writing, adult underwriting, and other instructional activities, providing them with the opportunity to demonstrate all aspects of their literacy knowledge. In this way, these instructional activities also serve as assessment opportunities, enabling me to observe the current phase of Albert's and Kevin's literacy knowledge and skills. When you understand phase theory or phase observation, you can loop together assessment and instruction and use both simultaneously to support your students in targeted and powerful ways. You can respond with one clear, step-by-step vision of how literacy unfolds by following the recommendations in this guide. Knowing how to respond based on phase observation will allow you to replace the conventional grab bag of isolated assessments and uncertain follow-up with principled assessment and targeted instruction.

What Is Phase Theory?

Children learn to read and write in *phases*. Their understanding of reading and writing evolves from minimal knowledge to letter knowledge to beginning letter/sound knowledge to writing and reading with one letter for a sound, until they finally learn to chunk letters in phonics patterns, which opens up the brain's express pathways to reading and writing. Each developmental phase reflects a constellation of expectations and accomplishments. In other words, once you identify a child's phase, you gain insight into other aspects of the child's reading and writing development, and then it's easy to pinpoint the child's needs and deliver targeted instruction. Identifying the child's phase of development creates a complete picture—or vivid snapshot—of what he or she likely knows or does not know at a given point in time about beginning literacy. This guide simultaneously surveys reading, writing, spelling, sound knowledge, fluency, vocabulary, and meaning to help you determine a child's phase of development. Phase identification allows you to focus on the specific skills that are important at a particular time in development, plan for instruction, and document the outcomes of your teaching by monitoring phase growth.

How the Guide Works

Step-by-Step Assessment Guide to Code Breaking: Pinpoint Young Students' Reading Development and Provide Just-Right Instruction provides a framework for what you are already doing to monitor each child's progress toward beginning reading and writing. It helps you know what to teach at the right time, recognize important signposts of development, and respond with appropriate instruction or intervention. The assessments are easy, child-centered, and mostly conducted during day-to-day, regular activity in the classroom. In fact, they're as easy as 1-2-3.

- **Step 1:** View the DVD clip as I model a 20-minute instructional and assessment session with two children, Albert at Phase 1 and Kevin at Phase 3. The DVD will illuminate the concept of phase observation and show how to link instruction, assessment, and intervention. These instructional demonstrations loop in assessment and reflective decision-making for determining the child's current levels of accomplishment and needs for moving forward.

- **Step 2:** Go to **Tab 1** to answer yes/no questions that help you match a child to his or her phase and focus on what's important for a particular phase. The guide zeroes in on the specific questions and answers that will help you monitor growth and make decisions for moving a student forward. Tab 1 reveals the big picture of the child's overall literacy development. (You may wish to take a practice phase-observation assessment by answering Tab 1/Phase 1, yes/no questions after viewing Albert or by answering Tab 1/Phase 3, yes/no questions after viewing Kevin. This optional practice activity clarifies exactly how phase observation works.) You may wish to reproduce the phase assessment sheets that match a child's level of development. Items marked "No" show parents' important learning goals their child needs to accomplish to help the child move forward.

- **Step 3:** Use the information in **Tab 2** to guide or provide deeper inquiry into your assessment, and use the information in **Tab 3** to decide what kind of instructional strategies, teaching techniques, or intervention you need to choose to move any child from his or her current phase to the next level.

Working With At-Risk Students

Knowing when various phase-related performance benchmarks are expected helps you to not only monitor phase growth but also to identify at-risk students who may not have demonstrated the minimal phase performance benchmarks one sees in children who are responding well to general education instruction in reading and writing by the expected time. This guide calibrates *minimal* expected phase performance benchmarks to the following key assessment periods:

- Beginning of kindergarten
- Middle of kindergarten
- End of kindergarten/beginning of first grade

- Middle of first grade
- End of first grade/beginning of second grade

It also allows you to calibrate to local mandates, high-stakes test requirements, and your local district's end-of-year performance expectations. Once you become familiar with phase observation, you will be able to predict end-of-year performance mandated by your school or district by tracking children's phase development. Figure 1 provides a baseline for expected accomplishment during phase development, and intervention guidelines for monitoring at-risk students. In each phase listed in Figure 1, if a child does not complete the phase and move into the next phase by the expected time, the child is at risk for failure with literacy development and needs small-group or intensive individualized instruction.

FIGURE 1

Monitoring for At-Risk Students

Phase 0—Expected in preschool
    Intervene if the child is not moving into Phase 1 by the beginning of kindergarten.

Phase 1—Expected between beginning and middle of kindergarten
    Intervene if the child is not moving into Phase 2 by the middle of kindergarten.

Phase 2—Expected between middle and end of kindergarten
    Intervene if the child is not moving into Phase 3 by the beginning of grade 1.

Phase 3—Expected from end of kindergarten to the middle of grade 1
    Intervene if the child is not moving into Phase 4 by the middle of grade 1.

Phase 4—Expected from the middle of grade 1 to the beginning of grade 2
    Intervene if the child is not in Phase 4 by the beginning of grade 2.

Note: *Many children reach the phases before the minimal expectations listed above.*

Step-by-Step Assessment Guide to Code Breaking: Pinpoint Young Students' Reading Development and Provide Just-Right Instruction helps you fine-tune the habit of close observation by showing what's important to look for at a particular phase of reading, writing, and spelling development. It's a growth model and progress-monitoring guide designed to help you pinpoint a student's or group's instructional needs at each phase of development and choose the right instruction at the right time. In this way, it's the perfect guide for both instruction and early intervention.

Phase Observation: Monitoring Operational Changes in Natural Literacy Development

Identifying a child's phase helps you see the strategic operations he or she is using and reveals where the child is in the precise developmental sequence that all children go through in learning to read and write. Simultaneously using multiple growth measures for reading, writing, and spelling, *Step-by-Step Assessment Guide to Code Breaking: Pinpoint Young Students' Reading Development and Provide Just-Right Instruction* enables you to identify what phase a child is in, compare it with what is expected, identify problems in development where they exist, recognize lack of preparation, and, if needed, provide early intervention.

Our assessment model is not only evidence-based, it's elegant in its simplicity. You simply track one clear path in every child's journey to literacy by following his or her passage through five phases of reciprocal reading, writing, and spelling development:

Phase 0: *Operations Without Letter Knowledge*

Phase 1: *Operations With Letters but Without Sounds*

Phase 2: *Operations With Partial Phonemic Awareness*

Phase 3: *Operations With Full Phonemic Awareness*

Phase 4: *Operations With Full Code and Chunking Knowledge*

The last phase makes automatic, mature reading and writing possible. Proficient young writers and readers are able to write independently, from their imaginations, using the same English coding system that adults use, and to read chapter books using virtually the same type of brain functioning that adult writers and readers use. Writing at Phase 4 is not accomplished with perfect spelling because conventional spelling is harder than reading and requires a great deal of word-specific knowledge. However, as children progress through the phases, you will see changes in how they invent spelling that will reveal how they use the English code. As children's spelling knowledge grows, use of invented spelling diminishes.

Rather than assessing how many items or parts of the system a child is using—such as the number of sounds or letters a child can recall in a minute, or whether he or she is doing some isolated skill such as the voice-to-print match—phase assessment starts with observing the child's literacy in context. You begin by observing the child using integrated and meaningful *systems* of beginning literacy that allow you not only to observe the child engaging in meaningful literacy activities, but also to observe what parts, components, or items of literacy are being used at a particular phase. For example, when you observe a 4-year-old at Phase 1 write his or her name, you may also observe interest in and motivation for writing, spelling skills, letter knowledge, letter formation, directionality, pencil grip, page positioning, print orientation on the page, knowledge or lack of knowledge of sounds—a veritable host of important aspects of early literacy development, all revealed in one simple, meaningful act. The good news is that much of the observation of meaningful systems consists of activities you already do in your day-to-day reading and writing lessons in the classroom. *Step-by-Step Assessment Guide to Code Breaking: Pinpoint Young Students' Reading Development and Provide Just-Right Instruction* simply gives you a vehicle for documenting what you are observing, for tracking the child's progress, and for making decisions about how to move forward. On page 8, you will find a list of meaningful literacy systems that we will be observing, which are chock-full of data documenting a child's development at various phases of code-breaking.

A Final Word About Integrated Systems of Functioning

The following quote from the companion to this guide, *Breakthrough in Beginning Reading and Writing* describes the advantage of observing children as they read and write in meaningful contexts.

In reading and writing assessment, the system comes first and the parts are an outgrowth of using it. It's the same with learning to ride a bike, catch a fish, speak the native language, or play a musical instrument. One starts by getting into the meaningful system. Kids get interested in it, want to do it, pay attention, try it out, notice the patterns, and when they mess up, they try to fix it. They do it over and over and get better at it. The parts come together from doing it. Some of the harder parts need more attention. Some of the parts become automatic. (Gentry, *Breakthrough in Beginning Reading and Writing*, 2007, p. 63)

Systems You Will Be Observing

Observing Meaningful Systems in Younger Beginners (3- and 4-Year-Olds):

- Name writing

- Writing one-word stories or phrase stories

- Five-word spelling checks (surveying the child's strategy for inventing spellings)

- Reading Level A text from memory

- Reading adult underwriting or early-language experience stories from memory

- Responding to adult underwriting

Observing Meaningful Systems in Older Beginners (5-, 6-, and 7-Year-Olds):

- Oral readings from the individual's book bag or browsing box (observing the child rereading books he/she has practiced)

- Observations from stories collected in the child's writing folder (observing writings from the child's current repertoire)

- Story writing and interactive writing (guiding and observing story writing in progress)

- Spelling assessments (observing the child invent spelling for unknown words on a spelling test)

Phase observation recognizes that both the integrated *system* and the *parts* of beginning literacy are important. Once we observe how a child is operating within a meaningful system like the ones in the box on this page, we will determine what phase the child is in, and then we can ask what parts, components, or items related to literacy we observe this child using.

Optional: Try a Practice Phase Observation After Viewing the DVD

So now we are ready to begin phase observation. To get in the swing, you may wish to view the DVD of 4-year-old Albert and 5-year-old Kevin and go to Tab 1 to answer as many yes/no questions as possible from this short video observation. Not only will you see how phase assessment works, but you will also be amazed at how much you know about the child's level of development based on this focused set of questions. When you are finished with the practice session, you will be able to go to Tab 1, quickly identify *any* child's phase, do an observation by engaging the child in meaningful systems analysis just like the one you viewed on the video, answer the targeted set of yes/no phase questions, and, finally, plan for appropriate targeted instruction or intervention by using the guidelines in Tab 2 and Tab 3. So let's get started!

TAB 1

Assess the Child, Find the Phase

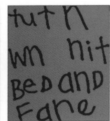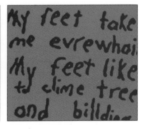

Helpful Hints for Monitoring Progress

Once you identify a child's phase, copy the pages for the appropriate Yes/No phase assessment that matches each child or download the appropriate forms from the DVD.

Color-code the Yes/No phase assessment as you mark it and note the date/dates an assessment is conducted. You may want to use the following color-coding system:

- Red-Beginning of Year Assessment
- Orange-Mid-Fall Assessment
- Blue-Mid-Winter Assessment
- Green-End of Year Assessment

Keep in mind that phase assessment may be conducted in part during regular guided reading and writing workshop lessons looping assessment with instruction and at other times during day-to-day observation of children in the classroom. The assessment need not be completed in one sitting and it doesn't require that the child be pulled out of instruction.

Use the same copy of the Yes/No phase assessment for the child until that child moves to the next phase.

Keep the phase assessment forms in the child's cumulative folder.

Use the Yes/No phase assessment to show parents learning goals for their child. (Learning goals are any items in a phase assessment marked "No.")

Over time, your phase assessments will be excellent records of each child's progress moving forward (or lack of progress) in reading, writing, and spelling.

Assess the Child, Find the Phase

Once you observe the child operating in several meaningful literacy systems just like the ones you observed in the video, determine which of the Key Operations (listed below) apply to the child.

Phase 0: If the child scribbles, is unable to write letters, and is unable to write his/her name,

Then he/she is Phase 0:   Go to page 12.

If the child can write his/her name and a few other important words, take notice of how the child invents spelling in story writing or in a spelling assessment.

Phase 1: If the child invents spelling in random letters,

Then he/she is Phase 1:   Go to page 14.

Phase 2: If the child invents a majority of his/her spellings with correct beginning letter-sound correspondences or partial letter-sound representations, such as HMT DPD for *Humpty Dumpty*,

Then he/she is Phase 2:   Go to page 18.

Phase 3: If the child invents a majority of his/her spellings using a letter for each sound such as KAM for *came*, NIT for *night*, TABL for *table*, and BABE for *baby*,

Then he/she is Phase 3:   Go to page 23.

Phase 4: If the child has stored many conventional spellings in memory and uses them in writing, and if the majority of his/her invented spellings include chunks of phonics patterns for each syllable, such as EVREWHAIR for *everywhere*, YOUNIGHTED for *united*, or SPESHIL for *special*,

Then he/she is Phase 4:   Go to page 27.

Predicting Phase Level from Reading Observations

Reading observations in the context of developing phases are a value-added support for running records, informal reading inventories, unit assessments, and standardized reading tests, putting each of these in the context of a developmental growth model. Note that phase assessment for reading may not be as exact for *identifying* phases as writing because reading is a less tangible record of how the child is thinking or operating. Because the teacher/observer can *see* writing, ponder it, ask questions, and take time to digest it, writing provides a visible record, and the child's operations are apparent. When supported by other reading assessments, however, observation of reading systems within phases is powerful and effective for monitoring the step-by-step sequence of code-breaking. It provides a wealth of information regarding how the child is functioning in reading fluency, comprehension, sight-word recognition, vocabulary, decoding, and other aspects of literacy development, allowing you to determine whether development matches what is expected at a particular phase.

If you are observing a reading system, follow these steps.

Key Operation 1: If the child is memorizing and rereading nursery rhymes and Level A text,

Then the child most likely is Phase 1:   Go to page 14.

Key Operation 2: If the child is memorizing and rereading Level A and B and sometimes C text,

Then the child most likely is Phase 2:   Go to page 18.

Key Operation 3: If the child is memorizing and rereading text at Levels B, C, and up through Level G,

Then the child most likely is Phase 3:   Go to page 23.

Key Operation 4:   If the child is reading much more independently and moving beyond Level G and higher,

Then the child most likely is Phase 4:   Go to page 27.

Three-Minute Phase Identifications and Jump-Start Questions

Sometimes a child's phase is almost immediately apparent. When you choose a system to observe, ask questions that will lead you to the child's phase quickly. Here are jump-start questions and key operations that identify the phase immediately.

Jump-start question: "Can you write your name?"

Phase 0:   If the child cannot write his or her name, he or she is Phase 0. (Go to page 12.)

Jump-start question: "What else can you write? Let's try a story or spelling check."

Phase 1:   If you see that all the child's invented spellings are random letters, he or she is Phase 1. (Go to page 14.)

Phase 2:   If you see that the child gets only the first letter correct when inventing a spelling, he or she is Phase 2. (Go to page 18.)

Phase 3:   If you see that the child almost always invents a spelling with one letter representing the sound and that he or she is spelling *all* the sounds in most words, rendering spellings such as KAM for *came*, NIT for *night*, ATE for *eighty*, or I WEL GIV U A KAN OPENR for *I will give you a can opener*, then he or she is likely Phase 3. Often the invented spelling is interspersed with correct spellings. (Go to page 23.)

[Note: View Kevin's Spelling Assessment in the DVD to see a perfect example of Phase 3 spelling.]

Jump-start question: "Can you spell some really hard words?"

Phase 4:   If you see that the child invents spellings in chunks, such as BOTUM for *bottom*, SPESHIL for *special*, TEMPEL for *temple*, LEVE for *leave*, GRATE for *great*, and intersperses these spellings with *many* words that are spelled correctly, then he or she is Phase 4 or higher. If you see that the child is an accomplished reader at second-grade level or higher and he or she reads with fluency and comprehension, he or she is likely Phase 4 or beyond—do a quick spelling check to verify, then go to page 27.

Phase 0: Operations Without Letter Knowledge

Phase 0

Key Operations

The child:

- Scribbles
- Cannot write his/her name
- Cannot invent a spelling

Critical Aspect

- Operations without letters

Expectations of a Phase 0 Writer

Check yes or no for the items observed.	Yes	No
Approximates letter writing	☐	☐
Attempts to express meaning through writing	☐	☐
Understands how writing works	☐	☐
Holds a pencil or pen properly	☐	☐
Positions paper properly	☐	☐
Orients print to the page	☐	☐
Uses nonalphabetic scribbles for writing	☐	☐

Note: If attempts are alphabetic, he/she is Phase 1 or higher.

Does not form letters	☐	☐

Note: If he/she does form letters, he/she is Phase 1.

Step-by-Step Assessment Guide to Code Breaking
© 2008 by J. Richard Gentry, Scholastic

	Yes	No
Does not invent spellings	☐	☐

Note: If there is evidence of invented spelling, he/she
        is Phase 1 or higher.

	Yes	No
Cannot write one's own name	☐	☐

Note: Lack of name-writing is an operational definition of Phase 0 (see Figure 2). Once a child
        can write his/her name, he/she is using letters and would therefore be Phase 1. Name-writing
        is an important step for moving children out of Phase 0 and into Phase 1.

FIGURE 2

Meredith's Phase 0 writing: 2 years, 4 months

Leslie's Phase 0 writing: 2 years, 6 months

Expectations of a Phase 0 Reader

Check yes or no for the items observed.

	Yes	No
Enjoys books	☐	☐
Has interest and confidence in reading	☐	☐
Has developed some book-handling concepts	☐	☐
Book orientation	☐	☐
Page-turning	☐	☐
Directionality	☐	☐
Approximates reading	☐	☐
Expects books to be meaningful	☐	☐

Expectations of Phase 0 Children With Sound Knowledge

Check yes or no for the items observed.

	Yes	No
Phonological Awareness:		
Can clap out syllables in names	☐	☐
Can shout out or otherwise designate rhyming words	☐	☐
Attempts to isolate beginning sound of his/her name	☐	☐

Phase 1 Assessment

Name _____ Grade _____

Dates of Assessment:

Phase 1: Operations With Letters but Without Sounds

Phase 1

Key Operations

The child:

- Writes with letters but without letter/sound knowledge
- Uses arbitrary cues for word-reading
- Invents spelling with random letters

Critical Aspect

- Nonalphabetic operations with letters

Expectations of a Phase 1 Writer

Check yes or no for the items observed.	Yes	No
Writes his/her name	☐	☐
Note: Name-writing with no sound knowledge is a defining operation of Phase 1.		
Writes using letters	☐	☐
Has the urge to write	☐	☐
Attempts to express meaning in writing	☐	☐
Understands how writing works	☐	☐
Uses letters to represent a message	☐	☐
Holds a pencil or pen properly	☐	☐
Positions paper properly	☐	☐

Step-by-Step Assessment Guide to Code Breaking
© 2008 by J. Richard Gentry, Scholastic

	Yes	No
Orients print to the page	☐	☐
Uses the alphabet, but no sound associations for writing	☐	☐

Note: If attempts are alphabetic, that is, if letters match sounds, he/she is Phase 2 or higher.

	Yes	No
Can name some letters (see Tab 2, page 32)	☐	☐
Can form some letters (see Tab 2, page 31)	☐	☐
Exhibits minimal to substantive alphabet knowledge	☐	☐

Note: Knowledge of the alphabet is one of the most important aspects of development for Phase 1. While all letters need not be mastered at Phase 1, growing letter knowledge facilitates the move to Phase 2. The charts on pages 31 and 32 in Tab 2 will help establish a quick assessment of the extent of the child's letter knowledge.

Check the item below that best describes the child's status.

Forms a few letters	☐ (Date: mo. __/day __ / yr. __)
Forms about half the letters	☐ (Date: mo. __/day __ / yr. __)
Forms most of the letters	☐ (Date: mo. __/day __ / yr. __)

	Yes	No
Can invent spellings with random letters	☐	☐
May show a preference for uppercase letters	☐	☐
May intersperse upper- and lowercase letters indiscriminately	☐	☐
May use numerals in invented spelling	☐	☐
May use impermissible spelling sequences such as double letters to begin a word	☐	☐
Can write one's own name and a few words	☐	☐
Illustrates stories from his/her imagination or experience and writes about them in words or phrases using random letters, as shown in Figure 3	☐	☐

Expectations of a Phase 1 Reader

Check yes or no for the items observed.

	Yes	No
Begins to memorize a few Level A easy readers	☐	☐
Reads back adult underwriting in examples such as those presented in Figure 3 (see page 16)	☐	☐
Reads leveled text selections from browsing box with fluency after practice	☐	☐
Retells leveled text selections from browsing box with understanding and appropriate vocabulary	☐	☐

FIGURE 3

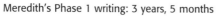

A flock of butterflies

Meredith's Phase 1 writing: 3 years, 5 months   Leslie's Phase 1 writing: 3 years

	Yes	No
Begins to make the voice-to-print match	☐	☐
Enjoys books	☐	☐
Develops more sophisticated print concepts	☐	☐
Book orientation	☐	☐
Page-turning	☐	☐
Directionality	☐	☐
(see Tab 2, page 33, Print Concepts)		
Begins to develop a lexicon of sight words stored in memory	☐	☐
Makes no systematic letter-sound matches	☐	☐
Logo matches are in evidence (e.g., McDonald's cued by golden arches)	☐	☐
Memorizes and rereads words and phrases	☐	☐
Learns to read a few words and phrases from memory	☐	☐
Words are stored in memory and recognized automatically	☐	☐
A few words	☐ (Date: mo. __/day __ / yr. __)	
Up to 30 words	☐ (Date: mo. __/day __ / yr. __)	

Expectations for Sound Knowledge at Phase 1

Check yes or no for the items observed.

	Yes	No
Demonstrates phonological awareness, such as clapping syllables	☐	☐
Demonstrates phonological awareness, such as shouting out or otherwise identifying the rhyme	☐	☐
Begins to respond to techniques such as hand spelling for identifying beginning sounds in some words	☐	☐
May begin progressing from easier to harder phonological awareness tasks (see page 55, "Tips for Teaching Sounds")	☐	☐

Phase 2: Operations With Partial Phonemic Awareness

Phase 2

Key Operations

The child:

- Writes using partial letter-sound matches
- Cues on beginning letters, making partial letter-sound matches for word reading
- Invents abbreviated spellings with partial letter-sound matches

Critical Aspect

- Demonstrates partial phonemic awareness

Expectations of a Phase 2 Writer

Check yes or no for the items observed.

	Yes	No
Increases the volume of writing	☐	☐
Increases ability to match letters to sounds	☐	☐
Moves toward mastery of letters	☐	☐
Expresses meaning in writing	☐	☐
Understands how writing works	☐	☐
Holds a pencil or pen properly	☐	☐
Positions paper properly	☐	☐

	Yes	No
Orients print to the page	☐	☐
Matches some letters to sounds when writing	☐	☐

Note: If attempts are fully alphabetic, that is, if letters match all the sounds, he/she is Phase 3 or higher.

	Yes	No
Can name most letters	☐	☐
Can form most letters	☐	☐
Generally exhibits substantive alphabet knowledge	☐	☐
Moves toward mastery in forming letters	☐	☐
Can invent spellings in partial alphabetic representations	☐	☐

Note: Partial alphabetic representations are a defining operation of Phase 2. If mostly full alphabetic representations are evident, that is, one letter for every sound in the word, then the child is in Phase 3.

	Yes	No
Increases knowledge of letters, graphemes, phonemes, graphophonemic associations, phonological/phonemic awareness, phonological recoding, and spelling patterns	☐	☐
Increases lexicon of sight words already stored in memory	☐	☐
May intersperse upper- and lowercase letters indiscriminately but with less abundance than at previous phases	☐	☐
Expands orthographic knowledge, such as recognition that doubled letters at the beginnings of words are impermissible	☐	☐
Illustrates stories from his/her imagination or experience and writes about them in words or phrases using partial phonemic awareness, as shown in Figure 4	☐	☐

FIGURE 4

Meredith's Phase 2 writing: 5 years old

Leslie's Phase 2 writing: 6 years

Expectations of a Phase 2 Reader

Check yes or no for the items observed.

	Yes	No
Continues to memorize easy-to-read books, working from levels A through C	☐	☐
Reads leveled text selections from browsing box with fluency after practice	☐	☐
Retells leveled text selections from browsing box with understanding and appropriate vocabulary	☐	☐
Reads back adult underwriting in examples such as those presented in Figure 4 (see page 19)	☐	☐
Continues to enjoy books and responds to a broader range of books through read-alouds	☐	☐
Stores lexicon of up to 30 or more sight words in memory	☐	☐

Note: The particular words a child might have stored in memory at Phase 2 depend upon which words he/she has been exposed to. Sight-word knowledge at this level may be very difficult to measure reliably and validly on timed tests or sight-word recognition tests because of a ceiling effect in the child's repertoire. When children at Phase 2 keep a word box or ring clip with sight words for collecting "Words I Can Read," these provide records of which words they know.

	Yes	No
Cues on partial alphabetic information (Ehri 1997; Gentry 2006)	☐	☐
Generally doesn't analogize independently unless given the pattern (knows *rat* but doesn't analogize to figure out a related unknown word such as *mat*)	☐	☐
Expands the repertoire of easy-to-read books, working from individual collections in book bags or browsing boxes	☐	☐
Memorizes and rereads words, phrases, and books, expanding the repertoire to reading several lines of text or more elaborate stories	☐	☐
Learns to read more words and phrases from memory	☐	☐
Stores more sight words in memory	☐	☐
Reads up to 30 or more word-wall words over time	☐	☐

Step-by-Step Assessment Guide to Code Breaking
© 2008 by J. Richard Gentry, Scholastic

Expectations for Sound Knowledge at Phase 2

Check yes or no for the items observed.

	Yes	No
Demonstrates phonological awareness, such as syllable awareness or recognition of rhyming words	☐	☐
Demonstrates partial phonemic awareness *Note: Evidence of partial phonemic awareness is a defining feature of Phase 2.*	☐	☐
Increases knowledge of letter-sound correspondence	☐	☐
Continues processing from easier to harder phonological tasks, achieving "yes" in some of the following categories (Yopp & Yopp, 2000):	☐	☐
Hand-spelling onsets and rhymes. (/J/ plus /-ack/ = *Jack*)	☐	☐
Matching. "Which words begin with the same sound?"	☐	☐
Sound isolation. "What sound do you hear at the beginning of *Jack*?"	☐	☐
Sound substitution. "What word would you have if you changed the /J/ in *Jack* to /b/?"	☐	☐
Blending. "What word would you have if you put these sounds together: /J/ plus /-ack/?"	☐	☐
Stores words in memory and recognizes them automatically	☐	☐

Use the chart in Figure 5 to help identify key letter-sound associations generally mastered in Phase 2. Check for single-consonant sound-symbol associations listed in this chart and note consonant-vowel-consonant (CVC) and consonant-vowel-consonant-silent *e* (CVCe) patterns.

Check yes or no for the items observed.

	Yes	No
Begins to develop phase-appropriate knowledge of phonics	☐	☐
Sound-symbol associations in Figure 5	☐	☐
CVC short-vowel patterns	☐	☐
A few CVCe long-vowel patterns	☐	☐

• *Note any letters or basic sounds that aren't known.*

FIGURE 5

Phonics Chart I: Key Sound-Symbol Relationships to Assess and Teach

a as in *bat*	g as in *goat*	o-e as in *home*
m	l	v
t	o as in *hot*	e as in *bed*
s	h	u-e as in *use*
i	u as in *cup*	p
f	b	w as in *wet*
a-e as in *cake*	n	j
d	k	i-e as in *like*
r	z	o-e as in *yoke*

Step-by-Step Assessment Guide to Code Breaking
© 2008 by J. Richard Gentry, Scholastic

Phase 3: Operations With Full Phonemic Awareness

Phase 3

Key Operations

The child:

- Writes using complete letter-sound matches
- Attends to full letter-sound matches for word reading
- Invents spellings with one letter for each sound in a word

Critical Aspect

- Full phonemic awareness; spelling patterns are not represented in chunks

Expectations of a Phase 3 Writer

Writer's invented spellings match a letter for each sound in the word, indicating full phonemic representation. (Many sounds are not represented conventionally.)

Check yes or no for the items observed.

	Yes	No
Increases the volume of writing	☐	☐
Writes meaningful independent pieces	☐	☐
Matches letters to all sounds when inventing spellings	☐	☐
Positions the paper appropriately	☐	☐
Exhibits substantive alphabet knowledge	☐	☐
Can invent spellings in full alphabetic representations	☐	☐

> *Note: Full alphabetic representations are a defining operation of Phase 3. If chunking is mostly evident, that is, if syllables are spelled in chunks of acceptable phonics patterns such as YOUNIGHTED for* united, *then the child is in Phase 4.*

	Yes	No
Increases knowledge of letters, graphemes, phonemes, graphophonemic associations, phonological/phonemic awareness, phonological recoding, and spelling patterns	☐	☐
May intersperse upper- and lowercase letters indiscriminately but with less abundance than at previous phases	☐	☐
Recognizes that doubled letters at the beginnings of words are impermissible (Wright & Ehri, 2007)	☐	☐
Writes with enough accuracy so that adult underwriting of stories may be phased out	☐	☐
Illustrates stories from his/her imagination or experience and writes about them using full phonemic awareness, as shown in Figure 6	☐	☐

FIGURE 6

Safety
in a Car
It showed a
mannequin. If it
didn't have
on its seat
belt, it
would fall
through the window.

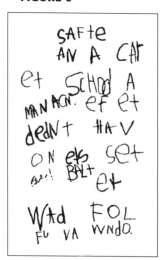

This is a pic-
ture for Mom.
I hope you
like this
pic-
ture of
Donald Duck
and Dais-
y Duck.

Meredith's Phase 3 writing: 5 years, 3 months   Leslie's Phase 3 writing: 6 years, 3 months

Expectations of a Phase 3 Reader

Readers cue on all the letters in a word. Memorizing and "rereading" likely moves beyond levels B and C and sometimes up through Level G and higher. Fluency is achieved from repeated readings and may include finger-pointing and word-by-word reading. Comprehension is apparent through retellings, interactions with text, and connection-making, as well as analysis and synthesis.

Check yes or no for the items observed.

	Yes	No
Memorizes Level C through Level G readers	☐	☐
Reads back adult underwriting	☐	☐

	Yes	No
Expands the repertoire of easy-to-read books, working from individual collections in book bags or browsing boxes	☐	☐
Reads leveled text selections from browsing box with fluency after practice	☐	☐
Retells leveled text selections from browsing box with understanding and appropriate vocabulary	☐	☐
Continues to enjoy books and responds to a broader range of books through read-alouds	☐	☐
Continues to increase lexicon of sight words already stored in memory	☐	☐
Stores lexicon approaching up to 100 or more sight words in memory	☐	☐
Cues on full alphabetic information (Ehri 1997; Gentry 2006)	☐	☐
Analogizes independently without being given the pattern (e.g., knows *rat* and can analogize to figure out a related unknown word, such as *mat*)	☐	☐

Expectations for Sound Knowledge at Phase 3

Check yes or no for the items observed.	Yes	No
Shows evidence of full phonemic awareness *Note: Evidence of full phonemic awareness is a defining feature of Phase 3.*	☐	☐
Has basic knowledge of single letter-sound correspondences	☐	☐
Continues processing from easier to harder phonological tasks, achieving "yes" checks on virtually all of the following categories (Yopp & Yopp, 2000):	☐	☐
Hand-spelling onsets and rhymes. (/J/ plus /-ack/ = *Jack*)	☐	☐
Matching. "Which words begin with the same sound?"	☐	☐
Sound isolation. "What sound do you hear at the beginning of *Jack*?"	☐	☐
Sound substitution. "What word would you have if you changed the /J/ in *Jack* to /b/?"	☐	☐
Blending. "What word would you have if you put these sounds together: /J/ plus /-ack/?"	☐	☐
Stores words in memory and recognizes them automatically	☐	☐

- *Note any letters or basic sounds that aren't known.*
- *Use Figure 7 to continue identifying key letter-sound associations generally mastered in Phase 2 and continued in Phase 3.*

Chart adapted from *The Literacy Map: Guiding Children to Where They Need to Be* (Gentry, 1998). These charts are based on Burmeister's research (1975), which identified a set of approximately 45 letter-sound correspondences that have a utility rate high enough to justify instruction.

Continue to focus on the following high-frequency sound-symbol relationships first. Check off items indicated on page 22 in Phase 3 and continue filling in the chart.

FIGURE 7

Phonics Chart I: Key Sound-Symbol Relationships to Assess and Teach

a as in *bat*	g as in *goat*	o-e as in *home*
m	l	v
t	o as in *hot*	e as in *bed*
s	h	u-e as in *use*
i	u as in *cup*	p
f	b	w as in *wet*
a-e as in *cake*	n	j
d	k	i-e as in *like*
r	z	o-e as in *yoke*

Phonics Chart II: Digraphs

Once the key letter-sound associations in Chart I are mastered, focus on the following, judging timing of focus on frequency of use.

ch as in *chip*	ou as in *cloud*	kn as in *knot*
ea as in *meat*	oy as in *boy*	oa as in *boat*
ee as in *need*	ph as in *phone*	oi as in *boil*
er as in *her*	qu as in *quick*	ai as in *maid*
ay as in *day*	sh as in *ship*	ar as in *car*
igh as in *high*	th as in *thank*	au as in *haul*
ew as in *new*	ir as in *girl*	aw as in *paw*

Phase 4: Operations With Full Code and Chunking Knowledge

Phase 4

Key Operations

The child:

- Writes using chunks of phonics patterns
- Attends to chunking for word reading
- Invents spelling in chunks of letter patterns

Critical Aspect

- Operations occur with knowledge of how the code works; spelling patterns are represented in chunks

Expectations of a Phase 4 Writer

Check yes or no for the items observed.

	Yes	No
Increases the volume of writing	☐	☐
Spells many words conventionally and uses chunks of acceptable phonics patterns when inventing spellings	☐	☐
Writes meaningful independent pieces	☐	☐
Invented spelling attempts are mostly in chunks of acceptable syllable patterns, with two-thirds or more of words in most pieces spelled correctly	☐	☐
Can invent spellings in full alphabetic representations and in chunks	☐	☐

Note: Full alphabetic representations are a defining operation of Phase 3. The Phase 4 child moves beyond Phase 3 and incorporates chunking, that is, syllables are spelled in chunks of acceptable phonics patterns, such as YOUNIGHTED for united.

	Yes	No
Uses spelling analogies, such as BOTE (analagous to *note*) for *boat*	☐	☐
Continues to increase knowledge of letters, graphemes, phonemes, graphophonemic associations, phonological/ phonemic awareness, phonological recoding, and spelling patterns	☐	☐
Spells at beginning second-grade level or higher	☐	☐
Continues to increase lexicon of sight words already stored in memory	☐	☐
Illustrates stories from his/her imagination or experience and writes about them in words or phrases using chunking as shown in Figure 8	☐	☐
Writes using elaborate story frames (see pages 59–60)	☐	☐

FIGURE 8

THES AFTERNEWN

it's going to rain.

It's going to be fair TOMORO.

"This afternoon it's going to rain. It's going to be fair tomorrow."

Paul's Phase 4 writing: 6 years, 1 month

My feet
are flesh.
I whair
sis 3.
My feet take
me evrewhair.
My feet like
to clime trees
and billdings
I walk to
school.
My feet
make me
swem in
water. My
feet are
tiyerd at
the end
of the
day

MY foot

Dan's Phase 4 writing: Grade 1

Expectations of a Phase 4 Reader

Check yes or no for the items observed.

	Yes	No
Reads Level G books and above, moving to independent reading without reliance upon rereading and memorizing texts	☐	☐

Step-by-Step Assessment Guide to Code Breaking
© 2008 by J. Richard Gentry, Scholastic

	Yes	No
Doesn't require adult underwriting except in cases where it might help English language learners	☐	☐
Stores lexicon well beyond 100 or more sight words in memory	☐	☐
Cues on chunking information (Gentry, 2006)	☐	☐
Analogizes independently without being given the pattern (e.g., knows *rat* and can analogize to figure out a related unknown word, such as *mat*)	☐	☐
Expands the repertoire of books including chapter books, working from individual collections in book bags or browsing boxes	☐	☐
Relies less on memorizing and moves to independent reading without having to practice reading books to commit them to memory	☐	☐
Stores more sight words in memory	☐	☐
Reads leveled text selections from browsing box with fluency	☐	☐
Retells leveled text selections from browsing box with understanding and appropriate vocabulary	☐	☐

Expectations for Sound Knowledge at Phase 4

Check yes or no for the items observed.	Yes	No
Shows evidence of chunking knowledge *Note: Evidence of chunking knowledge is a defining feature of Phase 4.*	☐	☐
Stores words and many common spelling patterns in memory and recognizes them automatically	☐	☐
Recognizes that different spelling patterns can represent the same sound, as in *e*, *ee*, and *ea* for long *e* in *be*, *bee*, and *beat*	☐	☐
Responds well to explicit spelling instruction *Note: Phase 4 students should be engaged in explicit spelling instruction, moving to a second-grade level or higher spelling curriculum.*	☐	☐

	Yes	No
Understands how to sort words according to phonics patterns	☐	☐

Note: Word sorting should be used to develop chunking knowledge and extend ability to analogize. Chunking knowledge should grow exponentially at Phase 4. Work includes high-frequency patterns and contrasts such as the bit/bite, fir/fire, mat/mate chunking patterns on page 42 in Tab 2. Observe and assess students' word-specific knowledge during word-sorting activities.

FIGURE 9

When my cousin
told me that she
had a rich dad
that surprised me.

TAB 2

Zero In on Needs: Tools and Guides

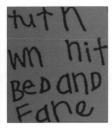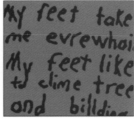

Zero In on Needs: Tools and Guides

Sometimes you need assessment instruments to help you inquire more deeply into a child's level of functioning. Think about how the assessments you already use coincide with each phase. Use the following Tab 2 assessment instruments and guidelines to enhance and fine-tune your inquiry.

Alphabet Knowledge

Use for Phases 0 to 1

Alphabet knowledge, which includes letter formation as well as letter naming, can be assessed informally and easily in the context of children's meaningful writing. You may monitor a child's growth of alphabet knowledge in day-by-day observation during writing workshop.

Letter Formation Checklist

Use for Phases 0 to 1

Put a check over each letter observed in the child's writing.

Uppercase Letters the Child Knows How to Write

☐ ☐
A B C D E F G H I J K L M N O P Q R S T U V W X Y Z

Lowercase Letters the Child Knows How to Write

☐ ☐
a b c d e f g h i j k l m n o p q r s t u v w x y z

You may use a quick "letter-writing check" to survey the child's ability to form letters by calling out the remaining letters at random. Example: "Can you make a *P*?" "Can you make an *R*?" "Make a *W*." "Make a *G*."

Check the item below that best describes the child's status.

He/she writes a few letters.	☐	(Date: mo. __/day __ / yr. __)
He/she writes about half the letters.	☐	(Date: mo. __/day __ / yr. __)
He/she writes most of the letters.	☐	(Date: mo. __/day __ / yr. __)

Letter-Naming Checklist

Use for Phases 0 to 1

Put a check over each letter the child can name when you point to it in his/her writing.

Uppercase Letters the Child Uses and Names in Writing

☐ ☐
A B C D E F G H I J K L M N O P Q R S T U V W X Y Z

Lowercase Letters the Child Uses and Names in Writing

☐ ☐
a b c d e f g h i j k l m n o p q r s t u v w x y z

You may use a quick "letter-naming check" to survey the child's ability to name letters by calling out the remaining letters at random. Example: "What is this letter?" (*P*) "What is this letter?" (*R*) "What is this letter?" (*G*)

Standardized Tests

Standardized forms of alphabet assessment are used or mandated in some schools or districts. Examples include the alphabet subtests of Clay's 2005 *An Observation Survey of Early Literacy Achievement*; Invernizzi, Meier, Swank, and Juel's 1999 *Phonological Awareness Literacy Screening* (PALS–Pre-K); and Good and Kaminski's 2002 *Dynamic Indicators of Basic Early Literacy Skills* (DIBELS). (McGee, L. in Paratore & McMormack, 2007) Phase observation will enhance your use and understanding of these tests, back them up, or provide documentation when these tests may not be an accurate measure of an individual's accomplishment.

An Observation Survey by Marie M. Clay

The following tests are recommended from *An Observation Survey of Early Literacy Achievement* (Clay, 2005)

- Running Records
- Letter Identification Test
- Concepts About Print Test
- Word Tests

Print Concepts

Print concepts include book concepts, directionality, one-to-one match between voice and print, and word, letter, and punctuation concepts. I have found the McGill-Franzen Print Concepts chart in Figure 10 to be a helpful and concise instrument for recording print concepts.

FIGURE 10

Print Concepts

Student _____ Teacher _____

Directions	Scoring and Concept Analysis	Date	Date	Date
Hand the book to the child with the book spine toward the child.	Put a check over the concept and the date mastered.			
Before opening the book, say: "Show me the front of the book."	Book Concepts			
	Front cover			
"Point to the title."	Title			
"Show me where you start reading."	Print carries the message (not illustrations)			
	Directionality			
"Which page do we read first?"	Beginning of text			
"Show me with your finger which way you would go when you read."	Left-to-right sequence			
"Show me with your finger which way you would go when you read."	Return sweep			
During reading, say: "Point to each word while I read." Observe whether the child points to each word as the teacher reads. Is there an exact match between number of words spoken (read) by the teacher and the printed words to which the child points?	One-to-one match between voice and print Observations:			
After reading, ask the child to use index cards to:	*Word Concepts*			
"Show me one word only."	One word			
"Show me the first word on this page."	First word			
"Show me the last word on this page."	Last word			
"Show me one letter."	*Letter Concept*			
"What is this?" [.]	*Punctuation Concepts* Period			
"What is this?" [?]	Question mark			
"What is this?" [!]	Exclamation point			
	Total Print Concept Points			

Fall book title _____

Winter book title _____

Spring book title _____

Total will be between 12 and 14, depending on punctuation in book you use.

(McGill-Franzen 2006)

Finger-Point Reading

Use for Phase 1 and Phase 2

Finger-point reading assesses whether a child is aware that a spoken word matches a written word in text. Check to see whether the child points to the word he or she is saying in a memorized text. This may be done with short nursery rhymes; rereadings of easy, leveled texts; or with adult underwriting. After children memorize the text, the teacher checks for finger-point reading as the child reads orally. Children who have the concept of what a word is will point to the word being said. Some references refer to this ability as voice-to-print matching. Morris and his colleagues have documented that ability to do the voice-to-print match is particularly important for Phase 2 because the child is stabilizing the concept that the printed word matches the spoken word. In doing so, the Phase 2 reader/writer eventually comes to the realization that words have beginnings and endings; then they realize that words have middle parts, too, and that these middle parts offer cues for reading (Morris, Bloodgood, Lomax, & Perney, 2003). Thus the voice-to-print match is very important in moving children from partial to full phonemic awareness, that is to say, from Phase 2 to Phase 3, and eventually leads them to pay attention to the middle parts of words, which research has shown are the hardest to read (Ehri, 1998; Lewkowicz, 1980; Morris et al., 2003). Phase 2 children start out paying attention to the beginning and sometimes the beginning and ending of words. Phase 3 children pay attention to the beginning, middle, and ending. Finger-point reading helps the beginner develop the concept of what a word is, thereby leading to recognition that words have beginnings, endings, and, later, recognition that there is something in the middle. This concept is critical for helping the child figure out how the code works.

Informal Assessment of Language and Vocabulary

We learn a great deal when we pay attention to the student's language use and vocabulary in both instructional and assessment interactions. McGee provides the following recommendations:

> *Teachers can also prepare informal vocabulary assessments by selecting a set of 10–12 vocabulary words that are particularly relevant to a theme or set of books to be used during a 2–3-week unit. Teachers select one or two book illustrations that provide opportunities for children to use many of these target vocabulary words or phrases and ask them to tell what is happening in the illustrations. Teachers note whether children use any of the target vocabulary as they talk about the book illustrations (Senechal, 1997). Alternatively, children can be asked to retell informational or storybooks as teachers check off a list of the target vocabulary words that children might be expected to use in their retellings (Leung, 1992).*

> (McGee, 2007, p. 76)

Informal Reading Inventories

Informal reading inventories are excellent instruments for assessing various reading accomplishments during phase development, including word recognition in isolation; independent, instructional, and frustration reading levels; comprehension; and reading rate. Teachers who understand and master informal reading inventory criteria for assessing students are able to apply these same criteria to measure word recognition, match children with appropriate texts, and assess comprehension and reading rates of children responding to curriculum materials such as leveled texts in day-by-day reading observations in the classroom. Samples of excellent informal reading inventories include *Basic Reading Inventory* (Johns, 1997) and *Informal Reading Inventory* (Burns & Roe, 2002). All reading teachers should be familiar with the implementation and use of informal reading inventories.

Guidelines for Phases of Reading Development

The summary chart in Figure 11 gives teachers a quick reference to the strategic operations, text materials, and text levels that are expected at a particular phase.

Comprehension: Assessing Story and Informational Book Retellings

Use for All Phases—Using Various Levels of Text

Teachers may use story and informational book retellings to assess comprehension at all phase levels. As the child moves to higher phases, the retellings are conducted with higher levels of text.

FIGURE 11

Phases of Reading Development

	Strategic operations	*Text materials/levels*
Phase 0 Nonreaders	*Readers do not notice letters.* • Name recognition • Recognition of environmental print • Scribbling • Attempted memorization of words and phrases	• Name tags • Labels • Environmental print • LEA charts • Nursery rhyme charts • Picture and poem charts • Caption books, board books • Big books *(continued on next page)*

FIGURE 11 Phases of Reading Development (*continued*)

	Strategic operations	*Text materials/levels*
Phase 1 Pre-alphabetic readers	*Readers do not use letters.* • Guessing • Cueing from pictures • Using arbitrary cues (golden arches to read *McDonald's*) • Remembering words as visual logo matches for word reading • No systematic letter-sound processing • Attention is paid to nonalphabetic information • Phonological awareness is possible (e.g., clapping syllables, recognizing rhyming words) • No phonemic awareness • Memorization of easy texts	• Name tags • Labels • Environmental print • LEA charts • Adult underwriting • Nursery rhyme charts • Picture and poem charts • Big books • Keep books, caption books, pattern books, alphabet books, pop-up books, board books, concept books (animals, colors, numbers, plants, shapes, and so on) *Probable reading level begins with environmental print, names, words, labels, and phrases and moves on to a few Level A easy books.*
Phase 2 Partially alphabetic readers	*Readers cue on beginning and ending letters and sounds.* • Form partial letter-sound representations • Pay little or no attention to medial vowels • Match some letters to sounds • Rely on rudimentary alphabet knowledge • Start using the voice-to-print match • Echo reading • Text memorization of Level A to Level C easy text • Rereading adult underwriting or LEA stories	• Adult underwriting • Nursery rhyme charts • Picture and poem charts • Big books • Keep books, pattern books, alphabet books, pop-up books, board books, concept books (animals, colors, numbers, plants, shapes, and so on) *Probable reading level is Level A to Level C easy books. Phase 2 readers greatly increase the number of books they can read from memory. By cueing on partial alphabetic information, they memorize text more easily than Phase 1 readers do.*

FIGURE 11 Phases of Reading Development (*continued*)

	Strategic operations	*Text materials/levels*
Phase 3 Full alphabetic readers	*Readers cue on full-word reading by paying attention to all the letters in words.* • Sound words out letter by letter: i-n-t-e-r-e-s-t-i-n-g (e.g., don't recognize chunks: in-ter-est-ing) • Pay attention to medial vowels • Match letters to sounds • Display full phonemic awareness • Analogize using word families • Greatly increase store of sight words • Decode new words, letter by letter • Use grapheme-to-sound cues extensively • Echo reading continues • Text memorization continues • Ability to decode increases	• Adult underwriting is dropped • Children read own writing as it is created • Fiction and nonfiction *Probable reading level is Level C to Level H. Phase 3 readers greatly increase the number of books they can read and flourish in material that helps them learn medial vowel patterns (especially CVC short vowels), word families, and chunks of phonics patterns for pattern recognition.*
Phase 4 Chunking readers	*Readers chunk in phonics patterns or recognize high-frequency one-syllable words as chunks in polysyllabic words—for example,* dig *and* in *in* indignation. • More words are processed automatically, rather than slowly and analytically from chunking letter-sound representations • Sense themselves as grown-up readers • Decode nonsense words—*dit, buf, fler* • Use chunks for graphosyllabic analysis • Less dependent on word walls for new vocabulary • Learn new vocabulary by reading independently • Read independently without the need to memorize text through repeated readings	• Fiction and nonfiction *Probable reading level is Level J to Level K or higher, including chapter books. Reading is much more proficient and fluent than it was at previous levels.*

FIGURE 12

Prompts for Reading Response

Name _____ Date _____

Story Title _____

Book Level _____

Where does this story take place? (*Setting*)

Who are the main characters? (*Characters*)

What is this story about? (*Plot*)

What is the problem in the story? (*Conflict*)

What part do you like best?

How did this story make you feel?

What was the surprise in the story?

Compare-and-Contrast Prompts

Who was the good character? Why do you think so?

Who was the bad character? Why do you think so?

Which _____ was bigger? How do you know?

Which _____ was smaller? How do you know?

Scoring Sheet

Setting:	Excellent	Good	Poor
Character Recall:	Excellent	Good	Poor
Character Development:	Excellent	Good	Poor
Events:	Excellent	Good	Poor
Plot:	Excellent	Good	Poor
Details:	Excellent	Good	Poor

Comments:

What text-to-self, text-to-text, or text-to-world knowledge references were made by the child?

Fluency

Use for All Phases

While counting words per minute has been attempted as a measure of fluency, at lower levels I prefer teacher judgment as the teacher observes the child reading a book that has been practiced from a collection in the child's browsing box. I developed the following informal scale to guide my judgments of fluency. The scale is applied to different levels of text at various phases, to readings at the child's independent level, or, at the lowest reading levels, to books or adult underwriting that the child has memorized after repeated readings. For example, at Phase 2 a child would eventually be expected to demonstrate fluent reading with Level C texts; at Phase 3 the same child would be expected to demonstrate fluent reading with Level G texts.

FIGURE 13

Relative Levels of Fluency

Reads accurately with appropriate speed, expression, and attention to punctuation (may point to words in phases up to the beginning of Phase 3).

Reads with moderate accuracy with relatively good speed and some attention to punctuation (may point to words in phases up to the beginning of Phase 3).

Reads with speed and accuracy without pointing to words (finger-pointing is expected up through Phase 2 but should drop out during Phase 3).

Reading is somewhat slow and halting, with little expression.

Reading is word by word with no expression or attention to punctuation.

Reading is extremely labored and not fluent.

In "Assessing Reading Fluency" (http://www.prel.org/products/re_/assessing-fluency.htm), Tim Rasinski provides the following Curriculum-Based Measurement/Oral Reading Fluency (CBM/ORF) Guidelines, which may be used for assessing fluency at Phase 4 and higher (see Figure 14).

FIGURE 14

Procedures for Measuring Accuracy and Rate in CBM/ORF

Find a passage(s) of approximately 250 words written at the student's grade placement. Submit the passage to a text readability formula to estimate its grade-appropriateness.

Ask the student to read the passage for one minute and tape-record the reading. Emphasize that the text should be read aloud in a normal way, and not faster than normal.

Mark any uncorrected errors made by the student. Errors include mispronunciations, substitutions, reversals, omissions, or words pronounced by the examiner after a wait of two to three seconds without an attempt or response from the student. Mark the point in the text the student has come to after one minute of reading.

Repeat steps one and two with two different passages (optional). If you choose to repeat the process, use the median or middle score for analysis.

Determine accuracy by dividing the number of words read correctly per minute (WCPM) by the total number of words read (WCPM + any uncorrected errors). This number will be a percentage.

Determine the rate by calculating the total number of WCPM and comparing the student's performance against the target norms in Figure 15.

FIGURE 15

Oral Reading Fluency (ORF) Target Rate Norms

Grade	Fall (WCPM)	Winter (WCPM)	Spring (WCPM)
1		10–30	30–60
2	30–60	50–80	70–100
3	50–90	70–100	80–110
4	70–110	80–120	100–140
5	80–120	100–140	110–150
6	100–140	110–150	120–160
7	110–150	120–160	130–170
8	120–160	130–170	140–180

Adapted from "AIMSweb: Charting the Path to Literacy," 2003, Edformation, Inc. Available at http://www.aimsweb.com/ norms/reading_fluency.htm. Data are also adapted from "Curriculum-Based Oral Reading Fluency Norms for Students in Grades 2 Through 5," by J. E. Hasbrouck and G. Tindal, 1992, Teaching Exceptional Children, 24, pp. 41–44.

The CBM/ORF approach to assessment [see Figure 14 for administration procedures], like the IRI, requires the reader to read grade-level text orally. However, the CBM/ORF only takes 60 seconds. During this period, the teacher or person administering the test marks the reader's uncorrected errors and then counts the total number of words read correctly (words read correctly per minute, or WCPM). Because the assessment is so quick, it can be repeated at one sitting on different passages. If multiple assessments are given, comparing the median (middle) score against performance norms is recommended.

An understanding of reading rate norms is necessary for using the CBM/ORF results accurately. Target reading rate norms based on several empirical data sources are presented in Figure 15. These norms suggest that reading rates tend to increase through the middle grades; however, the rate of acceleration diminishes after sixth grade. This suggests that although the automaticity component of reading fluency is a focus in the elementary grades, it should be nurtured and assessed even beyond these grades. (Rasinski)

Phonics: Record for Classroom Instruction

Single Letter-Sound Correspondences, Short Vowels, and a Few Basic E-Maker Patterns
Use for Phase 1, Phase 2, and Phase 3

FIGURE 16

a as in *bat*	g as in *goat*	o-e as in *home*
m	l	v
t	o as in *hot*	e as in *bed*
s	h	u-e as in *use*
i	u as in *cup*	p
f	b	w as in *wet*
a-e as in *cake*	n	j
d	k	i-e as in *like*
r	z	o-e as in *yoke*

Assess and teach key sound-symbol relationships, beginning with single letter-sound associations, short-vowel chunks, and CVCe long-vowel chunks.

Once the key letter-sound associations presented above are mastered, focus on the following, basing the order and time of presentation on frequency of use or occurrence in materials you are using for instruction.

FIGURE 17

Once the key letter-sound associations in Figure 5 are mastered, focus on the following, judging timing of focus on frequency of use.

ch as in *chip*	ou as in *cloud*	kn as in *knot*
ea as in *meat*	oy as in *boy*	oa as in *boat*
ee as in *need*	ph as in *phone*	oi as in *boil*
er as in *her*	qu as in *quick*	ai as in *maid*
ay as in *day*	sh as in *ship*	ar as in *car*
igh as in *high*	th as in *thank*	au as in *haul*
ew as in *new*	ir as in *girl*	aw as in *paw*

Adapted from The Literacy Map: Guiding Children to Where They Need to Be *(Gentry, 1998). These charts are based on Burmeister's research (1975), which identified a set of approximately 45 letter-sound correspondences that have a utility rate high enough to justify instruction.*

Phonics Record for Classroom Instruction: Chunking CVC and CVCe Matched Pairs

Use for Phase 3 and Phase 4

FIGURE 18

Consonant-Vowel-Consonant and Consonant-Vowel-Consonant-Vowel Matched Pairs

Use this list as an exercise in sight-word recognition. The goal is for the student eventually to recognize all 40 matched pairs automatically.

bit, bite	cub, cube	cut, cute
can, cane	cap, cape	cod, code
con, cone	Dan, Dane	dim, dime
fad, fade	fat, fate	fin, fine
fir, fire	hat, hate	hid, hide
hop, hope	kit, kite	Jan, Jane
man, mane	mad, made	mat, mate
not, note	pal, pale	pan, pane
pin, pine	rat, rate	rod, rode
rip, ripe	rob, robe	sit, site
Sam, same	Sid, side	Tim, time
tam, tame	tap, tape	van, vane
Tom, tome	tub, tube	win, wine

(Shaywitz, 2003, p. 214)

Assessing Invented Spelling in Writing and on Spelling Tests at Phase 3

Use for Phase 3

Look for the following features (see Figure 19) in invented spellings. If half of the invented spellings in a representative sample of the child's current work fit these patterns, the child is Phase 3.

FIGURE 19

8 Sound Features With Phase 3 Spellings

Sound Feature	What It Means	Sample Word	Phase 3 Spelling
tense vowels	long-vowel sound	eighty eat ice oak you	AT (letter name) ET IC OK U
lax vowels	short-vowel sound	bat bet bit cot cut	BUT (vowel shift) BAT BET CIT COT
preconsonantal nasal	*n* or *m* before a consonant	jump stamp	JUP STAP
syllabic sonorants	*l, m,* or *n* carries the vowel sound in a syllable	bottle atom open	BOTL ATM OPN
–ed endings	past-tense marker	stopped dimmed traded	STOPT DIMD TRADAD
retroflex vowels	*r*-controlled vowels	bird sister	BRD SISTR
affricates	sounds such as /jr/ and /dr/; /tr/ and /ch/	drag chip	JRAG TRIP
intervocalic flaps	sounds made by double *t*'s or *d*'s	bottle riddle	BOTL RIDL

Assessing Invented Spelling in Writing and on Spelling Tests at Phase 4

Use for Phase 4

Look for spelling patterns matching these samples (see Figure 20) in writing and spelling tests of Phase 4 students. If half of the invented spellings in a representative sample of the child's current work match these chunking patterns, the child is at Phase 4.

FIGURE 20

Sample Phase 4 Spellings

EGUL for *eagle*   OPIN for *open*

BANGK for *bank*   ABUL for *able*

MONSTUR for *monster*   LASEE for *lazy*

STINGKS for *stinks*   RANE for *rain*

TIPE for *type*   SAIL for *sale*

EIGHTEE for *eighty*   RIDDEL for *riddle*

TAOD for *toad*   BOS for *boss*

HUOSE for *house*   HOPP for *hop*

TAB 3

Target Instruction: Teaching Techniques

    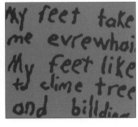

Target Instruction: Teaching Techniques

Phase theory is powerful because it enables you to make good decisions for providing the right instruction at the right time. If a child is in one phase, your focus may be A, B, C, but if he or she is in a different phase, the focus may be X, Y, Z. Each phase encompasses insights that spark an entire spectrum of understandings that you can then act on instructionally. The fine art of teaching literacy rests on knowing exactly which technique to use at which time.

The following instructional techniques and activities not only move students forward, but also allow opportunities for observations looping instruction with assessment. Think about how you can use the following meaningful literacy systems not only for monitoring progress but also for moving children forward.

Observing Meaningful Systems in Younger Beginners (generally 3- and 4-year-olds)

Name Writing

For teaching and observations of spelling, letter knowledge, letter formation, directionality, pencil grip, page positioning, print orientation on the page, knowledge of sounds

Wordless Picture Book Experiences

For teaching and observations of book handling, directionality, vocabulary development, comprehension

One-Word Story Writing or Phrase Story Writing

For teaching and observations of story planning, picture drawing and aural description, academic vocabulary, pencil grip, page positioning, print orientation on the page, invented spelling, letter knowledge, phonemic awareness, evidence of letter-sound correspondence, use of private speech, response to scaffolded writing

Adult Underwriting Sessions With Labels and Phrases

For teaching and observations of reading from memory, sight word recognition, voice-to-print match, concept of word, directionality, punctuation concepts, decoding and encoding strategies, making concrete connections between writing and reading, reading back writing of one's own ideas in a conventional form

Observing Meaningful Systems in Older or More Advanced Beginners (generally 5-, 6-, and 7-year-olds)

Readings From Collections Such as Book Bags or Browsing Boxes

For teaching and observations of reading level, fluency, comprehension, analysis, synthesis, voice-to-print match, sight word recognition, retelling, aural vocabulary, decoding strategies, text-to-text connections, text-to-self connections, text-to-world-knowledge connections

Story Writing

For teaching and observations of story planning, picture drawing and aural description, academic vocabulary, pencil grip, page positioning, print orientation on the page, invented spelling, letter knowledge, phonemic awareness, evidence of letter-sound correspondence, use of private speech, response to scaffolded writing

Adult Underwriting Sessions With More Advanced Writers in Phases 2 and 3

For teaching and observations of reading from memory, sight word recognition, voice-to-print match, decoding strategies, fluency

Spelling Assessments

For teaching and observations of letter formation, letter naming, determining the phase level, and documenting evidence of Phase 0–4 operations

Key Techniques for Moving Children From Phase 0 to Phase 1

Teach the child to write his or her name. Encourage picture drawing and story writing permitting the use of random letters. Lead children in letter formation and practice, wordplay with rhyming words, clapping syllables. Model elongating and enunciating sounds, particularly words that begin like the child's name.

Following five essential preschool practices linked to early achievement (Dickinson & Neuman, 2007; Neuman & Dickinson, 2002), Neuman and Roskos recommend engaging preschoolers and the earliest learners, including Phase 0 readers and writers, in practices such as the following:

- Reading aloud to children
- Shared reading
- Singing, rhyming, and playing with words
- Developmental writing
- Linking literacy to play
- Linking literacy to explorations of math, science, social studies, and art
- Use of alphabet songs and books

(Neuman and Roskos, 2007)

Neuman and Roskos provide the following toys, books, print, and writing/communication tool recommendations (see Figure 21) for preschoolers and children at Phase 0 and Phase 1.

FIGURE 21

Essential Literacy Materials for the Preschool Literacy Environment

Toys	*Books*	*Print*	*Writing/ Communication Tools*
• Magnetic letters • Alphabet blocks and puzzles • Puppets • Dolls of both genders, representing a variety of cultures • Open-ended play materials, salvaged from "real life" (old kitchen tools, old cell phones, egg cartons, fabric, paper tubes, laundry baskets, boxes) • Wood blocks and Duplo blocks • Collections of props for dramatic play (grocery store: brown bags, food posters, sign with store hours, pretend food; restaurant: place mats, play money, OPEN/CLOSED signs, aprons, order pads; transportation: luggage, travel brochures, tickets) • Dress-up clothes, play silks • Sorting and match letter cards • Sequencing cards • Word-making games, such as Scrabble	• ABC books • Big books • Books with predictable patterns • Rhyming books • Poetry • Nursery rhymes • Books with photographs • Fictional picture books • Informational books about science and nature • Picture dictionaries • Books stored in easily accessible bins, sorted by theme or genre, rotated frequently	• Functional sign-up sheets (such as library checkouts) • Alphabet chart • Classroom schedules and charts • Shared writing pieces, including children's own dictated words • Labels on objects around the room (e.g., door, shelf, table, chair, toy bins, storage containers) • Children's names displayed on lists, charts, and cubbies • Collections of printed materials that supplement dramatic play props (e.g., old checkbooks, business cards, menus, receipt books, event tickets, NO SMOKING signs, maps, store advertisements, WORK IN PROGRESS signs) • Posters that reflect children's interests (e.g., fine art posters labeled with title and artist's name) • Newspapers, magazines, catalogs, television guides • Song charts or cards	• A variety of jumbo crayons, pencils, pens, markers • A variety of paper (different sizes, with lines and without, construction paper, index cards, etc.) • Rubber alphabet stamps and ink pads • Stationery, envelopes, address book • Blank notebooks or journals • Portable writing materials, such as small chalkboards and chalk or small dry-erase boards and markers • Tape recorder and blank tapes to record children's stories or observations *(Neuman and Roskos, 2007)*

Using Alphabet Books

Appropriate alphabet books may be used beginning with Phase 0, continuing through Phase 2 and higher. McGill-Franzen (see Figure 22) recommends the following activities for guided practice with alphabet books.

FIGURE 22

Activities for Guided Practice with Alphabet Books

- Match letter cards to letters in alphabet books.
- Read aloud books, talk about how the writer represents the letters and sounds of the letters of the alphabet with children's names.
- Look in the library or online for alphabet books that offer a chance to explore:
  - alphabet name rhymes (like Mary Jane Martin's *From Anne to Zach*)
  - a songbook format ("*A*, you're adorable," "*B*, you're so beautiful. . .")
  - alphabetical photos paired with children's names (*My First ABC* by Debbie MacKinnon and Anthea Sieveking opens with "Allison's apple, Brian's book. . .")
  - alphabet riddles (for example, "You travel in this, it begins with an A. It starts on the ground, then flies up, up, and away. What is it?")
  - alphabetical labels and names (*All Around Kindergarten* by Christine Radow is one.)
  - favorite themes and alphabet (for example, there are ABC books on cars, farms, dinosaurs, monsters)
  - another culture (*Folks in the Valley* by Jim Aylesworth explores the Pennsylvania Dutch)
  - another language (*At the Beach* by Huy Voun Lee features a Chinese picture alphabet)

Some Other Teacher Favorites:

- *Alphabet City* by Stephen T. Johnson, which explores environmental print. (For example, a streetlight makes an *E*)
- *Animalia* by Graeme Base ("An armored armadillo avoiding an angry alligator")
- *Hurricane City* by Sarah Weeks ("Hurricane Alvin swept through town. . .")
- *Tomorrow's Alphabet* by Donald Crews ("A is for seed, tomorrow's apple. . .")
- *Into the A, B, Sea* by Deborah Lee Rose ("Into the A, B, Sea where Anemones sting. . .")

(McGill-Franzen, 2006)

Key Techniques for Moving Children From Phase 1 to Phase 2

Moving from Phase 1 to Phase 2, young children make a giant cognitive leap encompassing many aspects of literacy development. As shown in the quote below, this period of phase development involves new knowledge and accomplishments with multiple aspects and components of literacy, including letter knowledge, knowledge about sounds, a range of print concepts, sight-word development, and deeper overall knowledge about how printed words express meaning.

> *Key techniques for Phase 1 include participation in writing workshop, scaffolded writing, private speech, use of invented spelling, adult underwriting, hand spelling, modeling sound awareness by elongating and accentuating sounds in words, voice-finger pointing, modeling the voice-to-print match, teaching concept of word, and using word walls and other activities to help children begin to build a lexicon of sight words stored in memory.*
>
> *Scaffolded writing, private speech, and adult underwriting are particularly powerful techniques for Phase 1, and the kindergarten writing workshop offers daily opportunities for teaching and learning from their use.* (Gentry, 2007, p. 25)

Framing Stories, Scaffolded Writing, Private Speech, and Adult Underwriting

For Phase 0 Through the Beginning of Phase 3

Framing stories is what teachers sometimes do to help beginning writers select a story frame that is developmentally appropriate. For example, the child may give an elaborate oral description of the picture he or she has drawn of his or her classroom, but knowing that the child is capable of being successful only with a simple line story frame, the teacher might draw language from the child's oral description and suggest or frame the story as follows:

In My Classroom

Books

Pictures

Friends

To scaffold this piece, the teacher might go line by line, starting with the title:

_____ _____ _____

(Scaffold for "In My Classroom")

Once the child has "read the line" repeatedly to himself or herself as "in my classroom" (referred to as private speech), the child invents the spelling for each word. The teacher might complete the scaffold and have the child use private speech to rehearse "books, pictures, friends."

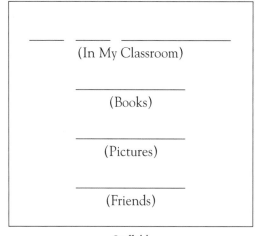

| Scaffold | Child Writing/Adult Underwriting |

After the child has completed the piece in kid writing, the teacher comes back and writes the same story in conventional English at the bottom of the page in the same line order and word order used by the child. This technique is called adult underwriting. Adult underwriting provides a conventional text that the child can now read back. The repeated reading and rereading of the adult underwriting allows the child to eventually memorize the piece that he or she wrote. Often these pieces are close matches in sophistication to the child's guided reading level.

Adult underwriting provides wonderful opportunities for reading back writing. Keep in mind that adult underwriting is presented in its entirety below the child's piece as opposed to writing the correct word under each invented spelling that the child wrote within the child's piece. The latter practice diminishes the integrity of the child's piece and makes reading back difficult and unnatural because the child's eyes would have to skip below the line under the invented spelling to read the correctly spelled word, and, of course, real reading doesn't work that way.

To recap, scaffolded writing is the drawing of lines to show the beginner where to put each word to be written—in effect, making a simple scaffold. Private speech is when the writer repeats words or a phrase to be written to give himself or herself auditory directions to support the mental action of writing the same words on the page (Bodrova & Leong, 1998). When used along with scaffolded writing, private speech is the repetition of the words to go on the lines and is a kind of rehearsal or planning stage for writing. It is often induced by asking the student to "read the lines" as you point to each line consecutively.

Reading Back Adult Underwriting (or Dictated Stories) From Memory

Adult underwriting provides the conventional version of a story the child has written so that the child can practice reading his or her own story writing. Anne McGill-Franzen writes about the power of having children read back their own writing:

> **Reads Back Writing:** *This is often the first actual—conventional—reading a child does. It is the easiest text for a child to read because it comes from him—both ideas and the printed message that communicates the ideas. The child draws a picture to represent what he is thinking, then uses what he knows about letters, sounds, words, and print concepts to create a written text that explains his drawing. By looking at his writing . . . we can see what he knows about words.* (McGill-Franzen, 2006, p. 102)

By providing the adult underwriting, the teacher helps the child connect writing and reading directly and allows inventive spellers at beginning phase levels to have exposure to a conventional English version of the story they write from their imaginations. With adult underwriting, readers see and reread an adult version of whatever they wrote, cueing on conventional text, which is easier to read and provides more cues than reading their own invented spellings.

Word Walls

Word walls may be started with Phase 1 students at the beginning of kindergarten to help them build a lexicon of sight words stored in memory and to provide words for writing. Organized by the alphabet chart, the kindergarten word wall differs from the more familiar first-grade word wall (Cunningham, 1995; Cunningham & Allington, 1994) in that two rather than five high-frequency words for reading and writing are practiced each week (Gentry, 2006). The chart on page 52 may help you choose word wall words for kindergarteners and first graders. Keep in mind that the words you choose should be high-utility words and include patterns that will give children access to analogous words.

Key Techniques for Moving Children From Phase 2 to Phase 3

The critical aspect for moving from Phase 2 to Phase 3 is to move from partial to full phonemic awareness. For each child, it's a move from attending to a few prominent sounds—beginning sounds, beginning and ending sounds, or sometimes partial spellings such as MTR for *motor*—to full phonetic representations of all sounds: MOTR. Many of the same strategies, therefore, used to move from Phase 1 to Phase 2 are employed to facilitate the child's move from Phase 2 to Phase 3, but the Phase 2 child has much more knowledge to work with—he or she knows more letter names, knows more sounds associated with letters, can do more manipulations with words and sounds, and knows more sight words from which to make associations, so he or she can now get complete representations for all sounds in words. The child is using similar systems and operations as at Phase 2 but with more completeness. He or she's now becoming equipped with enough knowledge to code all the sounds when writing a word or to pay attention to the middle part when reading a word. He or she's increasing the number of books he or she rereads from memory and moving to higher reading levels.

Particularly powerful techniques include finger spelling, which helps the child pay attention to all the sounds when writing a word, and word walls, which increase the words a child can read or write automatically and with which the child can make associations. Word families both greatly increase the number of words that the child is able to write and contribute to the child's ability to do more complex phonemic awareness activities such as sound substitution ("Change the *J* in *Jack* to /b/") and blending ("What would you have if you put /j/, /a/, /k/ together?"), and sound segmentation ("Tell the sounds you hear in *Jack*"). Use the three techniques together:

1. Stretch out the sounds in an unknown word.

2. Put each sound on a finger, starting with the thumb.

3. If the word has three sounds, use three consecutive boxes and place the letter in the box that represents the sound on each finger (see Sound Boxes on page 53)

FIGURE 23

200 Words Most Frequently Used in Children's Writing

Words are arranged in groups of ten from Group 1 to Group 20. The first group
(a *through* he) *lists the most frequent words that children use in writing.*

1	**4**	**7**	**10**	**13**	**16**	**19**
a	get	very	little	man	ran	never
the	there	play	know	Mom	only	girl
and	with	some	want	who	really	away
I	had	what	saw	tell	food	each
to	are	this	friend	over	sometimes	everyone
was	so	time	did	Dad	football	room
my	went	home	more	family	called	sister
of	up	going	see	name	father	any
we	at	good	big	next	something	teacher
he	said	as	us	night	took	that's

2	**5**	**8**	**11**	**14**	**17**	**20**
it	them	down	your	many	old	favorite
they	if	there	every	let	once	brother
would	her	house	didn't	eat	new	long
in	because	charge	dog	told	much	game
have	do	came	help	world	car	most
that	school	from	mother	right	into	cat
for	boy	friends	an	again	made	homework
you	his	to	also	try	run	game
she	about	other	around	way	years	thought

3	**6**	**9**	**12**	**15**	**18**	
be	day	after	started	well	team	
on	out	don't	now	love	kids	
but	him	our	think	off	always	
when	will	no	come	even	am	
me	not	just	take	thing	it's	
like	people	has	nice	work	wanted	
then	make	lot	first	class	found	
were	could	fun	best	where	bed	
all	or	things	put	boy	money	
go	can	by	how	another	why	

Smith, C. B., & Ingersoll, G. M., (1984). Written Vocabulary of Elementary School Pupils: Ages 6
and Above, *pp. 22–42. Bloomington, IN: Indiana University.* Monographs in Language and
Reading studies, *No. 6,* Adapted from Gentry, R., & Gillet, J. (1993). *Teaching Kids to Spell.*
Portsmouth, NH: Heinemann.

Sound Boxes for Words With Three Phonemes

(*See also Tips for Teaching Sounds, page 55*)

Key Techniques for Moving Children From Phase 3 to Phase 4

The move from Phase 3 to Phase 4 is a transition from providing a letter for each sound to spelling words in chunks of phonics patterns: MOTR BOT becomes MOTUR BOTE. Word reading also proceeds in chunks: in-ter-est-ing as opposed to i-n-t-e-r-e-s-t-i-n-g. Word family work and mastery of CVC short-vowel spellings greatly facilitate this move. Other important chunking patterns include the CV pattern in words like *my*, *by*, *me*, *he*, and *so* and the CVCe pattern in words like *bake*, *Pete*, *ride*, *hope*, and *cute*. Guided reading often includes word study, such as short-vowel study and high-frequency patterns such as *-ack* and *-ail* (*nail*, *mail*, *sail*, *tail*). Automatic recognition of upwards of 100 words gleaned from voluminous reading from browsing boxes and word wall work is extremely important.

Key Techniques for Moving Children From Phase 4 Onward

Phase 4 readers have enough knowledge of phonics patterns or high-frequency one-syllable words to chunk groups of letters or graphosyllabic constituents, transforming them into pronunciations and blending them to match words. The hallmark of Phase 4 is an understanding of the chunking system and the ability to bond spelling chunks to pronunciations and syllables in words. Phase 4 readers break polysyllabic words into pronounceable units. One-syllable words are recognized as syllable units in polysyllabic words. For example, *man* is recognized as a chunk in *manual*, *command*, *human*, and *dormant* and used for graphosyllabic analysis of polysyllabic words (Gentry, 2006, p. 179). Self-teaching while the child reads independently is more in evidence, with less need for explicit teaching of new vocabulary in activities such as word wall work. Children at Phase 4 are ready for explicit instruction in or above a second-grade level spelling curriculum.

Word Sorting

Word sorting is a core instructional strategy for developing chunking and word-specific knowledge in Phase 4 and beyond. It is a research-based way to develop automatic control of spelling patterns based on the fact that the brain learns to do things automatically by firing neurons over and over. Sorting words in particular patterns in teacher-led sorts, individual sorts, buddy sorts, speed sorts, and the like is hugely beneficial, allowing repetition to lead to automaticity with important patterns. As children sort word cards into columns based on spelling patterns, they engage in conceptual, hands-on, collaborative, student-friendly, theoretically sound, and empirically supported spelling instruction (Bear, Invernizzi, Templeton, & Johnston, 2000; Brown & Morris 2005; Gentry, 2004; Zutell, 1992, 1999). This brain-based sorting strategy helps Phase 3 and Phase 4 pupils develop word-specific knowledge for both writing and reading (Gentry, 2006).

Once Phase 3 pupils automatically recognize CVC patterns by sorting words such as *cap*, *hat*, *pet*, *hen*, *hop*, and *cut* or *put*, they move to a higher level, using sorting tasks to spell contrasting patterns such as *cap* and *cape*, *hop* and *hope*, and *cut* and *cute*. As they move to even higher levels, they move to automatic recognition and production of even more sophisticated variations on the same pattern as well as newly introduced patterns. Eventually students move from recognition and production of *hop* and *hope* to patterns of regularity such as *hopping* and *hoping* or *hopped* and *hoped*. By word sorting in an appropriate curriculum of word study for spelling, they establish and stabilize their word knowledge as it grows by degrees and in sophistication (Gentry, 2007).

Word sort options include the following:

Teacher-Led Sorts

Teacher-led sorts are an opportunity for the teacher to teach the pattern, to show how the pattern might contrast with another pattern, and to model how the sort is done. Once the teacher teaches a pattern, students might share in sorting the words under the direction of the teacher.

Individual Sorts

Students sort independently for individual practice. Phase 4 students might keep a notebook of patterns studied and write each sort in column formation. Writing the sort in column formation not only aids in the learning of the pattern but also serves as a record of which word sorts or chunking patterns a student has studied.

Buddy Sorts

Buddy sorts take advantage of the social context of learning and allow for repetition and practice under highly motivational circumstances. Buddy sorts greatly increase the number of times students engage with the unit pattern and lead to automaticity.

Speed Sorts

Speed sorting leads to automatic recognition and production of the spelling patterns being studied. Students may speed-sort individually, sorting a stack of word cards representing the target patterns as fast as they can, or they may compete against their classmates to see who can complete a sort most quickly and with the greatest number of words sorted correctly (Gentry, 2007). Focus on a variety of double-vowel patterns once a child enters Phase 4, such as *ea*, *ee*, *ay*, *oa*, *oi*, *ai*, and *au*.

Onsets and Rimes

Onsets and rimes are sounds that can be mapped to visual spelling patterns. In the word *back*, /b/ is the onset and /ăk/ is the rime. The onset is what comes before the vowel and the rime is the vowel and the rest of the chunk. Focusing on rimes is a good Phase 3 and Phase 4 activity. You may introduce the chunk with the hand-spelling technique when focusing on analogous spelling chunks in words such as *J-ack*, *bl-ack*, *sm-ack*, *wh-ack*, *tr-ack*, and so forth. Onsets and rimes have been shown to be important because they are the most psychologically accessible units of sound for mapping to spelling patterns (Goswami, 1996, p. 5). The 37 rimes presented below provide access to about 500 easy-to-read high-frequency words (Wylie & Durrell, 1970). For writers, these chunks have high utility for spelling by analogy (Cunningham, 1995). Rimes are particularly important at Phase 4 because of their utility for spelling analogies.

FIGURE 24

-ack	-as	-aw	-ice	-in	-ir	-ore
-ain	-ank	-ay	-ick	-ine	-ock	-uck
-ake	-ap	-eat	-ide	-ing	-oke	-ug
-ale	-ash	-ell	-ight	-ink	-op	-ump
-all	-at	-est	-ill	-ip	-or	-unk
-ame	-ate					

(Wylie & Durrell, 1970)

Tips for Teaching Sounds

The following information will help you match curricular expectations and the specific type and timing of instruction about sounds with the child's phase of development.

Phases 0 and 1: Teaching Knowledge About Sounds

- Clapping out syllables in words
- Shouting out or otherwise designating rhyming words in poems and nursery rhymes

To move children to Phase 2, use hand spelling as shown in Figure 25 to target beginning sounds (the onset in onsets and rimes).

FIGURE 25

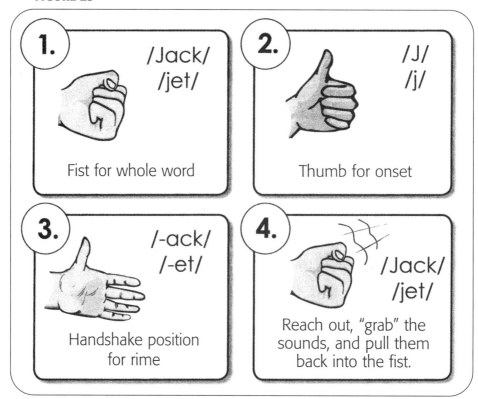

1. /Jack/ /jet/ — Fist for whole word

2. /J/ /j/ — Thumb for onset

3. /-ack/ /-et/ — Handshake position for rime

4. /Jack/ /jet/ — Reach out, "grab" the sounds, and pull them back into the fist.

Phase 2: Teaching Knowledge About Sounds

Note: *Yopp and Yopp suggest the following Phase 2 and Phase 3 progression from easiest to hardest phonemic awareness tasks, often moving along a continuum from less to more sophistication (Yopp & Yopp, 2000; reported in Gentry, 2006). Let these statements guide your teaching and focus for Phase 2 learners.*

- *Matching*: "Which words begin with the same sound?"

- *Sound Isolation*: "What sound do you hear at the beginning of *Jack*?" "What sound do you hear at the end of *Jack*?"

- *Sound Substitution*: "What word would you have if you changed the /j/ in *Jack* to /b/?"

- *Blending*: "What word would you have if you put these sounds together: /j/ plus /ăk/?"

- Model how to stretch out sounds in words.

- Use the hand-spelling technique illustrated in Figure 25 to focus attention on *beginning* sounds.

- Move from hand spelling with focus on beginning sounds to *finger spelling*, the same technique shown in Figure 25 but with a finger being used to represent each sound in a word. For example, for the name *Jack*: thumb up for /j/; pointer finger up for /ă/; and third finger up for /k/. The finger-spelling activity is effective for moving a child from Phase 2 (representing beginning and ending sounds) to Phase 3 (full phonemic representation), where the child makes a concrete representation for each phoneme. Repeat finger spelling, pausing after each finger is raised, and have the child write the letter that he or she thinks makes the sound in the letter boxes.

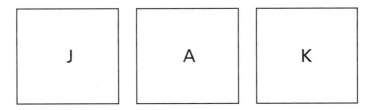

Sound Boxes—A Sample Phase 3 Spelling of *Jack* Based on Finger Spelling Representing One Letter for Each of the Three Phonemes

Phase 3: Teaching Knowledge About Sounds

- Sound Segmentation. "Tell me the sounds you hear in *Jack*."
- Sound Deletion. "Say *Jack* without the /j/." (/ăk/). "Say *Jack* without the /k/ at the end." (/jă/)
- Continue to use the finger-spelling technique to focus attention on all the sounds in a word.
- To move from Phase 3 to Phase 4, the child's attention moves from focus on the individual sounds (phonemes) in a word or syllable to focus on chunking patterns.
- Focus on recognizing word families: *bat, cat, mat, fat,* and so on.
- Focus on recognizing CVC as a chunk.
- Focus on recognizing CVCe as a chunk.
- Show children how to spell by analogies: if they can spell *pet*, then they can spell *bet, set, get,* and *let*.
- Focus on recognizing word wall words automatically as chunks.

Phase 4: Teaching Knowledge About Sounds

- Sort words with various spelling patterns.
- Practice hand spelling with focus on the rhyming chunks.
- Use hand spelling to focus attention on the chunk represented when the hand is in the handshake position (see Figure 25). For example, hand spelling may be used to help the child focus on different patterns for spelling the long-a sound (/ā/) in words such as *l-ay, m-ake,* and *n-ail*.

Matching Story-Writing Templates with Phases

There is a quantitative continuum for story writing, which matches roughly with phase development. While this continuum doesn't align directly with phase development and may not be used for determining a child's phase or assessing writing development, one generally observes particular quantitative levels of writing or story templates at particular phases. For phase assessment, it's helpful to know the length and type of story writing that is expected, or often observed, at a particular phase.

Note: The samples below are not fill-in-the-blank forms. Rather, they are intended to be templates of the type of phase-appropriate writing you normally see at various phases. All of these models cover an infinite range of topics and genres children may choose to write about.

Samples Often Observed at Phases 0 and 1

One-word stories and labels are often observed at Phase 0 and Phase 1.

One-Word Stories and Labels

Phase 0

Phase 1

Welcome Home

Samples Often Observed at Phase 2

One-word stories and labels are often followed by stories framed in phrases. Stories framed in phrases are often observed at Phase 1 and Phase 2. Sometimes Phase 2 writers can write using a few sentences and include some correct spelling.

Stories Framed in Phrases

7Up
milk
Raisin Bran
doughnuts

Humpty Dumpty

Phase 1

Phase 2

Samples Often Observed at Phase 2 and Phase 3

Stories framed in phrases are often followed by stories framed in sentences.

Stories Framed in Sentences

Example: I like _____ and _____.

A _____ ran over the _____.

| Phase 2 | Phase 3 |

Samples Often Observed at Phase 3

Stories framed in sentences are often followed by line stories, which often contain several sentences.

Line Story Frames

Line stories start at three lines and grow into about six lines. An example might be:

> My dog is mad.
>
> But I still like her.
>
> We play together.

Samples Often Observed at Phase 4

Line stories in sentences are often followed by elaborate story frames.

Elaborate Story Frames

Elaborate story frames may extend from many lines to several pages. Often they are developed in chunks or sections, allowing the writer to approach each section as a concrete unit and write the story chunk by chunk by chunk. To move a child from line stories to more elaborate pieces, introduce story frames such as beginning, middle, and ending. Give the child concrete instructions, such as using a separate sheet of paper for each section of the story: page 1 for the beginning, page 2 for the middle, and page 3 for the ending.

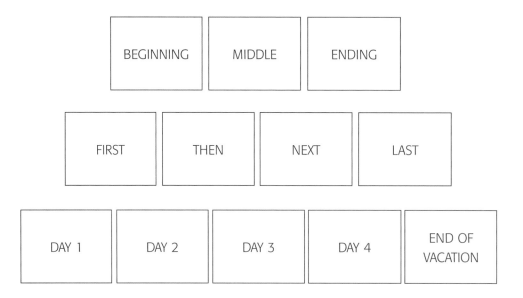

Matching Kids With Leveled Texts

Follow the Don Holdaway procedure of introducing books and reading them *for*, *with*, and *by* children (1979). Keep in mind that with each new phase, the child advances to higher levels of reading (see Figure 11 for Phases of Reading Development, page 35). Shared and interactive reading as well as reading and rereading instructional-level texts that are placed in the child's browsing box for repeated reading are encouraged until the student can handle the reading of the text independently. The books are often memorized at early levels. Rereading is particularly effective for phases 1 through 3.

Matching Texts for Independent Reading Level

- Child reads with very few errors (recognizes 95–100 percent of the words).
- Comprehension is high.
- Retelling is adequate or complete.
- Child responds appropriately to comprehension queries.

Five-Finger Test (Phase 3 and higher)

- Select a 100-word passage at random.
- Have the child read the section aloud.
- Hold up one finger each time the child misses a word.
- If the child misses more than five different words in the passage, the book may be too difficult for independent reading from the child's book bag.

Matching Texts for Instructional Reading Level

Use for guided-reading group work where the reader receives support from the teacher.

- Child reads with teacher assistance, eventually making few errors (recognizes 90–95 percent of the words).

FIGURE 26

Characteristics of Leveled Text

Levels A–C
Level 1–4

- consistent placement of print
- repetition of 1–2 sentence patterns (1–2 word changes)
- oral language structures
- familiar objects and actions
- illustrations provide high support

Levels D–E
Level 5–8

- repetition of 2–3 sentence patterns (phrases may change)
- opening, closing sentences vary
- or, varied simple sentence patterns
- predominantly oral language structures
- many familiar objects and actions
- illustrations provide moderate–high support

Levels F–G
Level 9–12

- repetition of 3 or more sentence patterns
- varied sentence patterns (repeated phrases or refrains)
- blend of oral and written language structures
- or, fantastic happenings in framework of familiar experiences
- illustrations provide moderate support

Levels H–I
Level 13–15

- varied sentence patterns (may have repeated phrases or refrains)
- or, repeated patterns in cumulative form
- written language structures
- oral structures appear in dialogue
- conventional story, literary language
- specialized vocabulary for some topic
- illustrations provide low–moderate support

Levels I–M
Level 16–20

- elaborated episodes and events
- extended descriptions
- links to familiar stories
- literary language
- unusual, challenging vocabulary
- illustrations provide low support

- Child is successful in the material with teacher assistance.
- Child accurately comprehends with some guidance.
- Retelling is adequate.
- Child makes logical predictions.
- Child can reread independently after guided reading.

The chart on page 61 of characteristics of leveled text (see Figure 26) is helpful in judging the level of a beginning text when the level is not provided by the publisher.

Remember that teachers of reading are lifelong learners. Your knowledge of techniques for moving children forward will continue to grow throughout your career. *Step-by-Step Assessment Guide to Code Breaking: Pinpoint Young Students' Reading Development and Provide Just-Right Instruction* is intended not only to help you form, or fine-tune, the habit of close observation by showing what's important to look for at a particular phase of reading, writing, and spelling development, but it will also provide an underpinning of sound theory and good instructional practices based on natural phases of development.

References

Bissex, G. (1980). *GNYS at WRK: A child learns to write and read*. Cambridge, MA: Harvard University Press.

Bodrova, E. & Leong, D. J. (1998). Scaffolding emergent writing in the zone of proximal development. *Literacy Teaching and Learning, 3*(2), 1–18.

Burmeister, L. (1975). *Words: From print to meaning*. Reading, MA: Addison-Wesley.

Burns, P. C. & Roe, B. D. (2002). *Informal reading inventory* (6th ed.). Boston: Houghton Mifflin.

Clay, M. M. (2006). *An observation survey of early literacy achievement*. Auckland, NZ: Heinemann.

Cunningham, P. (1995). *Phonics they use: Words for reading and writing*. New York: HarperCollins.

Cunningham, P., & Allington, R. (1994). *Classrooms that work: They can all read and write*. New York: HarperCollins.

Dickinson, D. & Neuman, S. B. (2007). *Handbook of early literacy research, Vol. 2*. New York: Guilford Press.

Ehri, L. C. (1997). Learning to read and learning to spell are one and the same, almost. In C. A. Perfetti, L. Rieben, & M. Fayol (Eds.), *Learning to spell* (pp. 237–269). London: Lawrence Erlbaum Associates.

Ehri, L. C. (1998). Grapheme-phoneme knowledge is essential for learning to read words in English. In J. L. Metsala & L. C. Ehri (Eds.), *Word recognition in beginning literacy* (pp. 3–40). Mahwah, NJ: Lawrence Erlbaum Associates.

Gentry, J.R. (1998). *The literacy map: Guiding children to where they need to be (K–3)*. New York: Mondo Publishing.

Gentry, J. R. (2006). *Breaking the code: The new science of beginning reading and writing*. Portsmouth, NH: Heinemann.

Gentry, J. R. (2007). *Breakthrough in beginning reading and writing: The evidence-based approach to pinpointing students' needs and delivering targeted instruction*. New York: Scholastic.

Gentry, J. R. & Gillet, J. W. (1993). *Teaching kids to spell*. Portsmouth, NH: Heinemann.

Good, R. H., III, & Kaminski, R. A. (2002). *Dynamic indicators of basic early literacy skills* (6th ed.). Eugene, OR: University of Oregon. Available at http://dibels.uoregon.edu.

Goswami, U. (1996). *Rhyme and analogy: Teacher's guide*. New York: Oxford University Press.

Holdaway, D. (1979). *The foundations of literacy*. Portsmouth, NH: Heinemann.

Invernizzi, M., Meier, J., Swank, L., & Juel, C. (1999). *Phonological awareness literacy screening (PALS-PK)*. Charlottesville, VA: University of Virginia.

Johns, J. L. (1997). *Basic reading inventory* (7th ed.). Dubuque, IA: Kendall/Hunt Publishing Company.

Leung, C. B. (1992). Effects of word-related variables on vocabulary growth through repeated read-aloud events. In C. Kinzer & D. Leu (Eds.), *Literacy research, theory, and practice: Views from many perspectives* (pp. 491–498). Chicago: National Reading Conference.

Lewkowicz. N. (1980). Phonemic awareness training: What to teach and how to teach it. *Journal of Educational Psychology*, (72), 686–700.

McGee, L. M. (2007). Language and literacy assessment in preschool. In J. Paratore & R. McCormack (Eds.), *Classroom literacy assessment* (pp. 65–84). New York: The Guilford Press.

McGill-Franzen, A. (2006). *Kindergarten Literacy*. New York: Scholastic.

Morris, D., Bloodgood, J. W., Lomax, R. G., & Perney, J. (2003). Developmental steps in learning to read: A longitudinal study in kindergarten and first grade. *Reading Research Quarterly*, 38(3), 302–328.

Moustafa, M. (1997). *Beyond Traditional Phonics*. Portsmouth, NH: Heinemann

Neuman, S. B., & Dickinson, D. K. (2002). *Handbook of early literacy research*. New York: The Guilford Press.

Neuman, S. B., and Roskos, K. (2007). *Nurturing knowledge: Building a foundation for school success by linking early literacy to math, science, art, and social studies*. New York: Scholastic.

Paratore, J. R., and McCormack, R. L. (Eds.) (2007). *Classroom literacy assessment: Making sense of what students know and do*. New York: The Guilford Press.

Peterson, B. (1998). *Characteristics of texts that support beginning readers*: Columbus, OH: The Ohio State University.

Rasinski, T. *Assessing Reading Fluency*. http://www.prel.org/products/re_/assessing-fluency.htm

Senechal, M. (1997). The differential effect of storybook reading on preschoolers' acquisition of expressive and receptive vocabulary. *Journal of Child Language*, 24, 123–138.

Shaywitz, S. (2003). *Overcoming dyslexia*. New York: Knopf.

Smith, C. B., & Ingersoll, G. M. (1984). Written vocabulary of elementary school pupils: Ages 6–14 (pp. 33–42). *Monographs in Language and Reading Studies*, No. 6. Bloomington, IN: Indiana University.

Wright, D. & Ehri, L. (2007). Beginners remember orthography when they learn to read words: The case of doubled letters. *Applied Psycholinguistics*, 28, 115–133.

Wylie, R. E., & Durrell. D. D. (1970, October) Teaching vowels through phonograms. *Elementary English Journal*, 47. 787–791.

Yopp, H. K., & Yopp, R. H. (2000). Supporting phonemic awareness development in the classroom. *The Reading Teacher*, 54(2), 130–143.